THE JOY OF YOUTH SPORTS

For more information on how to create a great sports experience for your child, visit:

WWW.INSIDEYOUTHSPORTS.ORG

THE JOY OF YOUTH SPORTS

CREATING THE BEST YOUTH SPORTS EXPERIENCE FOR YOUR CHILD

JEFFREY RHOADS

AVAPLAY PRESS

To James Jeffrey Abell

CONTENTS

INTRODUCTION

"Youth, with swift feet, walks onward in the way;
the land of joy lies all before his eyes."

... Edward G. Bulwer-Lytton

Like most human endeavors, the youth sports experience reflects the different wants of its participants. Fun, competition, winning, parental and peer acceptance, and self-expression can all drive a young athlete's desire to play sports. From their position, parents and coaches want their children to learn skills and lessons that develop self-esteem, confidence, and otherwise better prepare these young individuals for a full and successful life. Ideally, each child's journey through his or her years of youth sports provides a rewarding, joyful life experience.

Unfortunately, this journey is sometimes also filled with ignorance, excesses, and an obsessive focus on short term results that can irrevocably damage a young athlete's desire to participate in sports. An unhealthy emphasis on winning, negative coaching methods that destroy a young athlete's confidence, and over-involvement of parents, are but a few examples of potentially harmful behaviors.

This book presents an approach to youth sports that is centered on the principle that *all* young athletes should experience sports in a way that generates personal reward *and* a desire to continue playing. It puts forward a philosophy that emphasizes balance and growth—one that is supportive of the naturally athletic and less gifted child, the beginner and more advanced athlete, the children that will play competitively when older and those that will only play pickup games with friends.

This book is also about the joy of sports. Although other factors will motivate short-term participation, a sense of joy is essential to playing sports into later life (and obtaining the health and fitness benefits). For more competitive athletes, maintaining this feeling helps avoid the burnout that often accompanies more intense competition and training.

As a parent, you are your child's gateway to the world of sports. This book describes five steps that you can follow to provide your child with the best possible sports experience – the one that results not only in greater sports skills but also an increased sense of self-reliance, confidence, and an ongoing desire to participate. Some of these steps touch on coaching principles and methods. If you're coaching your child and others, this advice may directly impact your approach to coaching your team. As a non-coaching parent, you may have little influence over the methods used by your child's coach. But this information will help you identify and select the best coaches for *your* child.

I have come to these writings through a lifetime of playing, coaching and enjoying sports. From my first days of backyard baseball and football through my adult years playing basketball at the local YMCA, sports have helped fuel my enjoyment of life. I've coached youth basketball for over twenty five years and have worked with all levels of young players—including both absolute beginners with limited athleticism and more talented athletes who went on to success in high school and college. In both participation-based and competitive youth programs for younger and older children, the principles included in this book have proven themselves to work. For each child coached, of course, there is a parent. And from the experiences associated with this procession of children and parents over the years, I've gained insight into a wide range of sports parent behaviors—both positive ones that are supportive and negative ones that can undermine a child's development and self-esteem.

It is important to emphasize that the ideas and concepts contained in this book are universal ones that apply to any team sport and many individual ones.

I hope that you find wisdom in the words that follow. Whatever course you choose, my only wish is that each child is better for your efforts, enjoys his or her experience under your guidance, and wants to continue playing.

WHAT WE WANT
(FUN, LEARNING, LIFE SKILLS)

*"Success is not the key to happiness. Happiness is
the key to success. If you love what you are doing,
you will be successful."*

… Albert Schweitzer

This book is all about how parents can create an enjoyable, rewarding youth sports experience for their child.
Its contents will help provide you with the knowledge and
insight to achieve this goal.

The goal

So what makes up an ideal youth sports experience? And
can we really find a single path to success that encompasses
children of *all* skill levels and ability? Let's first start by
redefining our "best youth sports experience" goal to one
that is more specific. For each child, we want to:

- Maximize athletic abilities in a fun, positive learning environment

- Instill an enjoyment of sports and the desire to continue playing (ideally for a lifetime)

- Leverage the sports experience to develop life skills (leadership, responsibility, self-reliance, interpersonal relations)

This goal recognizes that each child is an individual with his or her own set of athletic abilities and potential. Affording every child the opportunity to "be their best," and doing so in a way that a child enjoys, is the key to a lifetime of benefits. Good health, the learning of important life skills, and a stronger sense of community head the list of benefits that can accrue to the adult who participated in a positive sports experience as a child.

A great youth sports experience

With this goal in mind, let's take a look at the elements that make up a successful youth experience. These include fun, skill development, heroic moments, increased self-esteem and self-reliance, community, and winning.

Fun

Playing sports provides many rewards—some that are generated internally and others that come from external sources. The most important internal reward for a child participating in sports is FUN. This feeling comes in different forms—from the simple joy of running around to more complex variations that embody team play and competition. Besides the immediate gratification of engaging in an enjoyable activity, fun is an essential ingredient for long term participation. Although a child may have talent and compete well, the absence of fun will likely lead a child to quit when other external rewards (praise, recognition, etc.) are no longer present.

Skill development

Learning and mastering new skills is essential for a child to have the necessary tools to participate, contribute, and compete. Although running around and casually playing a sport may provide fun with similarly minded children, more rewards and opportunity to play exist for children who have learned and mastered fundamental sport skills. One such reward is the self-confidence that is gained from an understanding of how to play a game and do it well.

Heroic moments (and glorious defeats)

Sports are attractive partly because of the various feelings they evoke. Besides fun, there is also the "thrill of victory" and the "agony of defeat." Heroic moments and glorious defeats are an essential part of the youth sports experience. They come together as a package deal—you can't have one without the other. They impart upon children the potentially lifelong satisfaction of rising up to meet a challenge, and sometimes the heartfelt disappointment of a failed opportunity. Either way, these emotions add depth to a child's life experience.

Self-esteem and self-reliance

As a child learns new skills, gains experience, and progresses toward a clearer understanding of how to play a sport, the child's confidence naturally grows. This, in turn, leads to an increased sense of self-esteem (satisfaction in oneself). The child becomes more self-reliant, understanding that he or she individually commands tools that can affect the outcome of a game. A child's self-reliance also increases as the child begins to organize and manage his or her *own* pickup game (a skill not cultivated within the adult-run games typical of youth leagues).

Community

A child who participates in sports shares with other participants the game and its values. This is most evident in team sports, where success is usually dependent upon the contributions of each team member. But individual sports also provide a sense of community. Shared values are present in all sports.

Community is also present in the bond that ties together athletes of all ages and generations. Young athletes feel the same joy and appreciation for sports that their parents, grandparents, and coaches experienced when they were young.

Winning

And finally, winning is part of a successful youth sports experience. Viewed with proper perspective, winning is an essential and required reward for continued participation. Everyone likes to experience their fair share of games where the final score favors them. But there are different ways to define "winning"—especially in participation-based youth sports. Those glorious defeats, where an individual or team competes courageously against a vastly superior team, do mean something. Improving one's individual performance, regardless of others' performance, is a "win." And when it comes to winning the battle of lifelong participation, these other types of victories are often the ones that really matter.

FIVE STEPS TO SUCCESS

*"Success is peace of mind that is the direct result
of self-satisfaction in knowing you did your best to
become the best that you are
capable of becoming."*

... John Wooden

Now that we've defined our goal and have a better grasp of what constitutes a successful youth sports experience, let's tackle the specifics of how we actually make it happen. Five steps are listed below that will ensure the positive outcome we want.

1. *Balance self-directed play and organized sports*
2. *Emphasize internal rewards*
3. *Use roles to create individual paths to success (but teach everyone everything)*
4. *Build from the bottom up*
5. *Set the stage for a lifetime of participation*

The multiple roles of parents

Parents often play multiple roles within youth sports including team coach, supportive fan, as well as personal advisor, coach, and provider. The above steps touch on these different roles to varying degrees. For example, step one (*Balance self-directed play and organized sports*) relates to the environment in which a child experiences sports – a factor that is largely controllable by each parent. On the other hand, step three (*Use roles to create individual paths to success*) is oriented more toward youth coaches.

Whichever role you play, you will benefit from understanding all five steps. Parents not involved in youth coaching will more fully know what they should look for in their child's coach. In the coaching-oriented steps you will also find ideas on how you, in your supportive parental role, can communicate the right messages to your child.

Every child benefits

It's important to understand that these five steps help form the underpinnings of a youth sports experience that benefits *every* child—regardless of the his or her natural ability. They promote a fun learning environment filled with opportunity for every child to develop athletically, gain life skills, and appreciate the internal rewards of playing sports that can fuel a lifetime of healthful participation.

So that you can better understand how to enhance the quality of your child's sports experience, let's now walk through each step in more detail.

STEP 1:
BALANCE SELF-DIRECTED PLAY AND ORGANIZED SPORTS

"You've got to be very careful if you don't know where you're going, because you might not get there."

... Yogi Berra

Up until the last two decades, it was not unusual to drive down a suburban or city street and see a number of kids playing a pickup game of baseball, basketball, or football. A number of societal changes (fewer stay-at-home moms, busier lifestyles, increased safety concerns, air-conditioned homes, more electronic distractions) have occurred since then and neighborhood games are now much less prevalent.

Organized sports dominate

Organized youth sports programs run by adults have taken over the typical child's sports life. Beyond the fundamental benefits of participating in sports (fun, fitness, community, etc.), these adult-run programs offer children other excellent benefits including:

- *Expert instruction.* Youth programs are often filled with dedicated, caring volunteer coaches who understand the sport they coach (and how to teach it).

- *A safe, structured learning environment.* Run by adults within a formal organization, most youth programs are geared first to the safety of the participating children. These programs usually have established guidelines that help promote a fun learning environment.

- *Formal competition.* Practices and other goal-directed preparation, officials, coaches, a "clock", can all make for a more exciting competition.

- *Relationships with adults.* Children gain experience interacting with adults, developing interpersonal skills that will benefit them later in life.

- *An opportunity to make new friends.* Organized sports often draw children together from different locations and backgrounds. This added diversity can help broaden a child's outlook on people and life.

In a generation of busy parents, and with the benefits listed above, it's no surprise that organized sports have now taken on a much larger role. Scheduled, highly structured, and safe, organized sports fit into today's lifestyle. Why not expect that organized sports can be the beginning and end of your child's sports experience?

The downside of organized sports

Unfortunately, this shift in emphasis toward adult-run programs has a downside, depriving kids of the important benefits inherent to the traditional neighborhood game.

It's vital to understand that neighborhood pickup games are much more than just playing sports. They're also about learning how to interact with other children—*without the help of parents or other adults.* These neighborhood games, organized by the children themselves, teach kids how to recruit, organize, and manage their games, helping them to develop self-reliance and relationship skills. They also let kids structure their games for the type of fun *they* want and need. Depending on the mix of players and their mood, the games can emphasize either relaxed fun or more serious competition. But importantly, the kids control their own experience—learning to become more self-reliant.

Although organized sports provide excellent benefits, they do not typically provide the former ones.

Organized youth sports programs also face their own problems—ones that can diminish your child's experience in sports. A limited number of volunteer coaches with varying degrees of expertise, multiple age groups and skill levels bunched together into single leagues, and different attitudes regarding how to balance fun and competition, all make it difficult to produce a program that fully satisfies the needs of every participant. As a result, complaints arise that programs are too competitive, do not provide equal playing time, and fail to give younger beginners and less-skilled children the best opportunity to learn and have fun.

Provide opportunities for self-directed play

As a parent, you should encourage your child to participate in neighborhood games and create opportunities for these games to occur. Don't simply outsource your child's sports education to an organized youth sports program.

Even in the more complex changing world we now live in, you still control your choices. Place limits on "electronics" time and send your child outside to play with other neighborhood children when possible. City, suburb, and rural neighborhoods all present different safety issues and potential risks. Only you can determine how much risk you are willing to assume. But ask yourself, "Is your neighborhood really any more unsafe than the one you grew up in— or has our omnipresent 24-hour news cycle simply sensitized our society to the *potential* dangers?"

If you're reluctant to send your child out into your neighborhood unsupervised, try to find a facility where your child can play with others in a self-directed setting. For example, it's not unusual in the afternoon at the local YMCA to see younger children involved in either a fun two-on-two pickup basketball game or a more competitive full court game.

You should always seek a healthy balance between parental involvement and providing your child with the freedom to explore sports on his or her own. Organized sports are only one part of the equation.

A Balanced Youth Sports Experience

- *Peer relationships*
- *Self-determined fun*
- *Game management (recruiting, arguments)*
- *Self-reliance*

- *Expert instruction*
- *Safety*
- *Formal competition*
- *Adult relationships*
- *New, diverse friends*

Self-Directed Play
(Pickup games)

Organized Sports
(Adult-run programs)

STEP 2:
EMPHASIZE INTERNAL REWARDS

*"The reality of the building does not
consist in the roof and walls, but
the space within to be lived in."*

… Lao-tsu

A child's motivation to play sports arises from both internal and external rewards. Internal rewards are ones that are intrinsic to the activity itself—the feelings within us that are evoked when we engage in a certain behavior. Examples include the satisfaction a child gains from mastering a new skill or performing to personal expectations, the thrill of participating in a close contest, the joy from running around and expending physical energy, the warm sense of belonging (to a larger group who share similar values), and while playing, experiencing the "flow" that comes from an expanded awareness and living in the moment.

External rewards have their place, but...

External rewards, on the other hand, are ones that come from outside the activity—usually from another person. These external rewards can be either abstract or concrete. For example, praise received from a parent or coach for performing a certain behavior well is an *abstract* external reward, as is an excessive focus on the scoreboard and winning. Treating a child to an ice cream cone after a good game is an example of a *concrete* external reward.

Both internal and external rewards play a role in motivating an athlete. At more competitive levels of play, external rewards such as playing time, public and peer recognition, scholarship offers, and money all can drive training and performance to higher levels. In youth sports, and especially with beginners, parental praise often plays an important role. It helps motivate a child to play sports at a time when his or her skill level doesn't generate the necessary internal rewards. Similarly, trophies and wearing "cool" uniforms are external rewards that can motivate a young athlete's interest in sports.

But external rewards also have a downside. Too much emphasis on these types of rewards may cause a young athlete to lose sight of the intrinsic motivators associated with playing the sport. And when the external rewards disappear, so does the child's desire to participate.

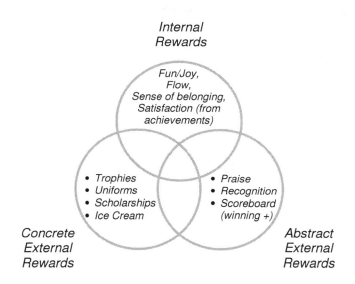

Internal
Rewards

Fun/Joy,
Flow,
Sense of belonging,
Satisfaction (from
achievements)

- Trophies
- Uniforms
- Scholarships
- Ice Cream

- Praise
- Recognition
- Scoreboard
  (winning +)

Concrete
External
Rewards

Abstract
External
Rewards

Helping your child experience the internal rewards

Although external rewards may help a child achieve greater success in the short run, it's the internal rewards that will drive the child's life-long appreciation and enjoyment of sports participation. As a parent, you should:

- Seek out coaches who not only teach technique, but also help elicit an understanding in your child of the internal rewards and benefits of participating in the sport.

- Lessen excessive parental praise, criticism, or other external parental influences that can dull your child's joy of participation and sense of self-reliance.

- Promote opportunities for your child to enjoy unstructured and self-organized play (neighborhood pickup games).

- Play catch with your child or engage in some other family sports activity (one with fun, friendly competition). Consider extending the family dinner time to include these activities.

Emphasize the internal rewards and use external ones only when required.

USE ROLES TO CREATE INDIVIDUAL PATHS TO SUCCESS

"What is a weed? A plant whose virtues have not yet been discovered."

... Ralph Waldo Emerson

Every child wants to be successful. As a youth coach or involved parent, your goal is to enable each child to achieve this outcome.

At the individual level, you can teach a player the fundamental skills they need to participate and compete. You can easily frame the child's mastery of a skill relative to his or her age, experience, talent, or past performance to provide a relative sense of positive progress and success. Doing so is especially helpful to beginners.

Meaningful roles

Team sports can provide beginners with many opportunities to experience positive, successful moments. But it often takes a good coach to set the stage for these moments to happen.

By assigning to a player a *team role*, one that is within his or her ability to perform well, the player can experience individual success by *meaningfully* contributing to the team's success. For example, in youth basketball, a coach can assign a smaller beginner to a guard position and instruct the child to set a screen when the point guard dribbling the ball approaches his or her defender. At the lower levels of youth basketball, this simple screen often leads to a layup and two points. Upon hearing the coach's congratulations for "making the play happen," the beginner knows that he or she played an important *role* in the team's success. The result is increased self-esteem and a broad smile on the child's face.

Beyond the earliest age groups, every team in every sport has its scorers, defenders, and "glue" players. By carefully evaluating a player's initial skill set, age, and physique, a coach can determine the team roles best suited to each player—the ones that can bring immediate success for both the individual and team.

Teach everyone everything

If you're a youth coach, look to expand a child's role as his or her ability grows. Don't limit potential. In practice, teach everyone everything. Also look for realistic opportunities in practice and games to challenge a child's abilities.

Try to find opportunities for your players to occasionally step beyond their primary role. In many sports, it's easy to move a child from one position to another during a game.

Although a child may lack the skills to play a position well, let him or her try. Pick moments that provide the child with a better chance to succeed (when the other team is playing its weaker players, for instance).

You can even find opportunities for your least skilled beginners to play a key position. For example, toward the end of a one-sided basketball game, you might rotate a different player into the point guard position each time down the floor. Make sure that everyone on your team is in on the fun, and they understand that you're not concerned about the inevitable turnovers.

Finally, you will face game situations in a close contest where you must decide whether to insert, or substitute for, a weaker player. Sometimes, the right choice may be to provide a less talented or inexperienced child with the chance for his or her big moment—one that may last a lifetime.

Evaluating your child's coach

As a parent, observe your child's coach and how he or she teaches the younger and seemingly less-talented players. Are the coach's teaching techniques in line with those described above? Do you sense that the coach is giving these children opportunities to succeed? Don't necessarily equate equal playing time with opportunity—a good coach will recognize the situations in which young players can best succeed and grow.

How you can help

If a coach does not positively frame your child's team role, then you will need to do so. Cast your child's contributions in the proper light. Explain how differences in age or experience may make it more difficult to excel now. Emphasize how small contributions can make a huge difference in a close game. Try to show your child how a certain physical limitation (small in stature) can often translate into a positive attribute (quick, and strong). And always remind your child that his or her physical body is constantly changing and that this change can lead to new opportunities.

A child who has an understanding of his or her capabilities, and grasps the concept of playing a team role, will always find acceptance within that sport's community of players. Even with limited physical talent, these children can enjoy the benefits of playing sports—and do so well into their adult years.

BUILD FROM THE BOTTOM UP

*"If you want to make a living flower, there
is only one way to do it—you will have to
build a seed for the flower and then let it,
this seed, generate the flower."*

... *Christopher Alexander*

This is an essential, guiding principle you must follow to create a successful youth sports experience for your child. Whether you're a youth coach or non-coaching parent, you should view youth sports as a developmental journey with each point on the way dependent upon having first reached the prior milestone. This voyage is characterized *not* by a single game or a one-lap race, but instead a progression of connected events occurring over the long course of a child's youth.

Start with a solid foundation

To play and enjoy any sport, a child must master fundamental individual and team skills. This always happens within the context of the child's physical capability and maturation. Certain skills are dependent on more fundamental ones while also requiring a minimum physical ability. Teaching the proper techniques at the appropriate time is crucial to a young athlete's development.

For example, making a three-point shot in basketball requires both good shooting form and the physical strength to generate the necessary force. The typical ten-year-old boy rarely has the physical strength to reach the basket from the three-point line, and if he does, the "shot" is more likely a throw. But from ten feet, this same boy can easily make the basket—and do so using the correct technique that will sooner enable him to consistently convert longer shots as his body matures.

Building a strong foundation as part of a well-constructed house is accepted wisdom. But just as some builders use inferior materials and construction techniques to more quickly and less expensively reach their goal, some coaches and parents do the same with their child's youth sports experience. And like poorly constructed buildings that fall apart in harsh weather, the child's game does the same in more challenging circumstances. Worse, the same child often turns away entirely from sports activities and their potential benefits.

Find the *right* programs and coaches

As a parent, search for the organized youth sport opportunities that match both your child's current abilities and physical makeup. Programs that challenge (but not overwhelm) your child are the ones you want. Especially at earlier ages, find the coaches and instructors that concentrate on individual and team fundamentals. Note whether the coach teaches to each player's current level, emphasizing the information that each player can use and apply. Instructing a beginner on an advanced technique (using sports jargon that he or she is unfamiliar with) is usually ineffective and a waste of everyone's time.

Youth coaches: build your team throughout the season

If you're a youth coach, you face the challenge of trying to develop *each* player's individual and team skills. In a team sport, you will also want to build within your players the understanding that they are an integral part of a shared team experience. None of this happens by itself, but is instead the result of you adding one layer at a time to each child's education.

Evaluating players

How do you actually go about doing this? As discussed in the prior topic, start by carefully evaluating your players' current skills and considering the roles that each player can successfully play. Also try to recognize each player's near-term *potential* talent. With proper coaching and instruction, these players can rapidly learn new, valuable skills and contribute to your team in a way you didn't initially envision.

Start slow—finish strong

After evaluating your players, establishing initial roles and considering possible future ones, you will need to prepare for practices and your first game. Prior to your first game, you must provide your players with the essential team information they need to compete. Establish your team's basic offense and defense and possibly discuss a few game situations. Keep it simple and make choices that are beneficial to your team and players *in the long run*—you are laying the foundation and should not strictly focus your instruction on winning that first game. Avoid gimmick strategies and tactics.

As your season unfolds, teach your players new skills and team play—always building upon your prior teachings. Help your players understand how the simple fundamentals connect to more advanced skills and how this, in turn, leads to both individual and team success. Build connections. Start slow, finish strong.

Develop every player

Coaches should attend to *all* of their players. In youth sports programs that emphasize equal participation, remember that much of your team's "win-loss" success depends on developing your beginners and less skilled players. Besides assigning straightforward tasks that these players can do well and build upon, act as a cheerleader to highlight their smallest successes. This is especially helpful early on for those children who are shy, introverted, afraid, or may have low self-esteem. When failures occur, use these moments to teach a positive lesson.

Don't shortchange your more talented and experienced players. Provide these children with the instruction and opportunities *they* need to succeed. These players may enjoy competition and have a strong desire to win. In some game situations, it may be appropriate to give your better players more playing time—just as other situations may dictate that you play your less talented players more. Equal playing time over the course of an entire season is often a better development approach than necessarily providing equal playing time within each game.

As a youth coach, it's your responsibility to take your group of players, nurture and develop their individual abilities, determine the roles that each of them can best play, and meld the parts into a whole. Do it the right way and you will provide *every* player with a strong sense of personal satisfaction and individual growth, an opportunity to enjoy a warm bonding experience with his or her teammates, and a season filled with many victories. And more importantly, your players will walk away wanting to play again.

STEP 5:
SET THE STAGE FOR A LIFETIME OF PARTICIPATION

*"We don't stop playing because we grow old;
we grow old because we stop playing."*

... George Bernard Shaw

One of the more disappointing statistics related to youth sports is that the drop-out rate increases substantially when children reach high school. A study by the Women's Sports Foundation in 2008 found that sports participation by high school students declines 25% after 5th grade. Other studies have shown an even higher drop-out rate. The primary reason given by children for dropping out was "not having fun." Alternative activities abound in the teen years and responsibilities and time commitments only increase as each child becomes an adult. Yet the need to maintain one's health and physical condition does not change. Mountains of research have shown that we benefit from physically active lifestyles.

The adult fun factor: sports versus "machines"

As adults, we can stay in shape through basic fitness activities that include aerobics, calisthenics, lifting weights, riding a bike, and running. To make our fitness regimens more efficient, we often use a variety of exercise machines at the local club. Although some may find these activities fun, the high drop-out rate of new fitness club members suggests otherwise. Even when adults know they need to exercise to stay healthy, they do not. Why? No fun.

Sports are an inherently more complex and satisfying fitness activity than simple exercise routines. Sports combine exercise, competition, strategy, and the opportunity to socialize—all within a single activity. They are the ultimate multi-tasking opportunity for today's busy society. A motivation to perform better within a given sport also encourages participants to independently exercise and use those fitness machines. Sports should be the best solution for engaging adults in a lifestyle of physical fitness.

So why don't we see more adults participating in sports?

The youth sports connection

Studies show that youth sports activities influence adult leisure time physical activity—both positively and negatively. A child who truly enjoys sports will likely continue playing as an adult, while the child who "fails" and drops out is less likely to do so.

Adolescent drop-out rates and a low level of adult participation in sports clearly indicate a problem exists. And if there is a connection between youth sports and adult participation, then we need to take a closer look at the youth sports experience. We need to identify the factors that impact this childhood experience—the ones that eventually determine whether an individual will enjoy participating in sports throughout his or her lifetime.

Let's first look at one key factor that can ultimately damage a child's desire to participate in youth sports.

The hurtful side of youth sports

A significant part of the problem is that our society places too great an emphasis on sports as a vehicle to achieve goals unrelated to the enjoyment of the activity itself. External rewards are pursued while internal ones languish in a secondary role. These external rewards are attractive. Success in sports leads to increased social status—for both the athlete and parent. A successful athlete may win a valuable college scholarship. And for some parents, youth sports provide an opportunity to live vicariously through the accomplishments of their children.

None of these external rewards, however, are a prescription for our youth to embrace sports in a way that leads to a lifetime of participation. Instead, they can lead to distorted practices that eventually diminish a young person's interest in sports. Here are some examples of possible negative outcomes:

- Specializing in a single sport at too early an age causes burnout and overuse injuries.

- Pre-pubescent stars physically mature into average athletes who no longer find enjoyment in sports without their earlier success and attention.

- Children who played for their parent's acceptance or with a "must-win" attitude fail to appreciate the intrinsic rewards associated with *playing* their sport.

- Super-competitive, driven high school and college athletes are unable to find enjoyment in sports as they age (and can no longer play at the highest level).

- Children are not exposed enough to sports (tennis, golf, volleyball) that they can enjoy throughout their lifetime.

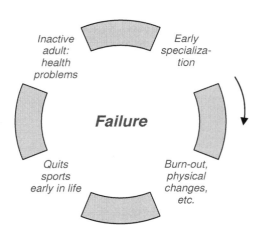

Inactive adult: health problems

Early specialization

Failure

Quits sports early in life

Burn-out, physical changes, etc.

A better path

If you accept that lifetime participation in sports is important, then you may need to adjust your parental perspective relative to youth sports. You can start by thinking of youth sports as a general education rather than preparing for a specific career.

Multiple sports—less specialization

First, expose your child to multiple sports throughout his or her early years and avoid specializing in a single sport. Although early specialization may be appropriate for a rare prodigy such as Tiger Woods, it is not so for almost every other child.

In addition to causing burnout and overuse injuries, focusing too early on a single sport removes potential crossover benefits from other sports. Early specialization also removes the opportunity to experience other sports that may be a better fit when the child's body and mind matures. Specialization reduces the opportunity for children to enjoy a wider range of great youth sports experiences—the ones that create memorable, satisfying moments.

By encouraging your child to play multiple sports, you provide a solid foundation for a lifetime of sports participation. Developing a more well-rounded set of athletic skills and knowledge enables your child to more easily adapt to whatever adult sports activity interests him or her later in life.

Expose your child to adult-friendly sports

Keep in mind that certain sports are simply more conducive to adult participation—either from the physical aspect or their availability. Adults can play racquet sports (tennis, platform tennis, racquetball) and golf throughout most of their lifetime. Pickup basketball games at the local YMCA or other public facility are commonly available to adults. Softball and volleyball leagues are more plentiful than adult football games. By exposing your child to these other sports, you are providing the general education which will pay dividends of enjoyment down the road.

Understand the process

And finally, the first four steps covered in this book are also an important part of the path toward lifetime participation. They help forge a holistic experience that promotes success and protects a child's enjoyment of sport. Understand the process, and the role you and your child's coaches play in it. Provide the fertile ground necessary for your child's sports participation to remain vital throughout his or her life.

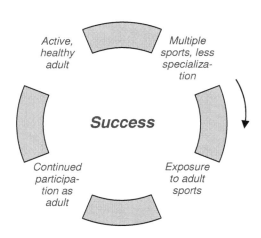

Active, healthy adult

Multiple sports, less specialization

Success

Exposure to adult sports

Continued participation as adult

WHO MAKES IT HAPPEN?
(IT TAKES A TEAM)

*"Learning is a treasure that will follow
its owner everywhere."*

... Chinese Proverb

As a child progresses through his or her years of youth sports, many people help forge the final product. Coaches, parents, and other children all play their part. Ideally, good coaches teach, caring parents provide support, and players eagerly pursue learning their sport.

Complementing the more organized efforts of coaches and parents are the child's own interactions with his or her circle of sports-playing friends. Whether it's a neighborhood pickup game or self-directed play in some other setting, children learn invaluable lessons from these types of games.

As already touched upon, coaches and parents have the potential to create either a good or bad youth sports experience. Let's look more closely at the roles played by each participant and specific practices that will help ensure a positive experience.

1) Coaches as teachers

The quality of a child's experience in organized youth sports is highly dependent on his or her coach. Good coaches both understand their sport and how to communicate this knowledge.

In our own education, most of us have experienced the teacher who was very knowledgeable—but unable to express information in a clear, concise way. We sometimes were left confused, unable to connect the dots to achieve a solution. Likewise, we may have been exposed to the personable, good communicator who we sensed lacked an in-depth knowledge of the subject taught. Knowledge and communicative ability—each by itself is insufficient. Although coaches may use different instructional techniques and emphasize different aspects of the game, they must be knowledgeable teachers with an ability to communicate.

As a parent, your goal is to try to find coaches who demonstrate these traits. Word-of-mouth recommendations from parents, direct observation, and feedback from other kids can help you determine the coaches who are the best fit for your child. "Tough" coaches may be appropriate for your more competitive and confident child while coaches who employ a softer, more supportive style may help your younger beginner find his or her way. But whatever the style, the coach must first be a good teacher—one who can communicate his or her expertise.

Teaching the game's values

Besides being a good teacher of a sport's individual and team skills, the exceptional coach also teaches his or her players how to *enjoy* the game. This enjoyment comes from many sources, not the least of which is an appreciation for the values of the game—those intrinsic qualities that keep drawing a child back to playing a sport.

An exceptional coach both creates and recognizes moments to highlight these values. He or she may purposefully set up a competitive situation in practice, enabling players to meet and surpass some challenge—and in the process, to help evoke within them important character traits such as perseverance, selflessness, self-control, integrity, fairness, self-confidence and leadership. Practice drills can be more than simply a lesson on skill development. Fun drills and contests can also spark a child's mind toward a richer experience in sports—one that is filled with passion, self-expression, creativity, and excellence.

Likewise, during a close, exciting contest, a coach may briefly pause and remind his or her players of the moment's meaning. Or possibly the coach asks a question—like the one Marv Levy, former head coach of the Buffalo Bills famously posed to his football players, "Where would you rather be than right here, right now?" This type of coach invites his or her players to look deeper, beyond winning and external rewards—to also appreciate the intrinsic joy of playing the game.

Throughout practices and games in team sports, the exceptional coach also recognizes opportunities to create bonds of responsibility and caring between players as they pursue a shared team goal. Moments of team success *and* failure can strengthen these ties. Respect for the game (and all of its participants) is another essential lesson that must be conveyed.

In youth sports, "teaching moments" abound. An excellent coach uses all of them.

On positive coaching

As mentioned above, coaches have different personalities and approaches to instructing their players. But in organized youth sports—and especially participation-based leagues—a coach should use a "positive" teaching style. Here are some key elements in this coaching approach.

- *Believe in your kids – expect improvement.* For each child under his or her tutelage, the exceptional coach sees opportunity for growth. This coach does not accept the child's ability as fixed, but instead recognizes the areas in which the child may eventually excel. He or she can see how certain attributes (size, quickness) are compensatory—providing success in areas other than the ones in which they present a more obvious weakness.

  This coach sees the entire spectrum of ability, both existing and latent, and is able to find ways in which each child can succeed. The exceptional coach believes in each child and the child's potential to find enjoyment in playing the sport. And most importantly, each child begins to incorporate this belief into his or her own sense of what's possible.

- *Use positive language to sandwich criticism.* Whenever possible, a coach should use the "sandwich" technique while instructing. A coach should first encourage the player on what he or she was doing right; next, state the problem; and finally, indicate what action or behavior the player should have taken [what was done right – the problem – best action].

For absolute beginners, struggling younger players, and children with more sensitive personalities, soften the criticism and emphasize the positive. Older, more experienced players, on the other hand, respond well to constructive criticism—especially when they understand that you appreciate their talent and have higher expectations for them.

- *Frame difficult situations as either an opportunity or lesson learned.* Practices and games in youth sports are filled with failure. Overmatched beginners, players having less athletic ability, and teams missing key components, will all struggle against superior opponents. From a purely win-loss perspective, there are lots of losers.

  But the exceptional coach breaks down each contest into smaller ones, finding opportunities for each player to succeed. For example, during a basketball practice, a coach might have his players run a "Suicide" race where each player progressively touches lines further down the court, always returning to the starting baseline. On most teams, there are children of different ages, sizes, and athletic ability. There are always one or two children who will win the race and a couple of other children who will usually finish last. Although this drill may help the kids' conditioning and appeal to the fastest ones, it's not inherently fun for the slower ones. But by shouting words of encouragement to these children, giving attention, and casting the race as one against another player of similar ability, the coach can get these players' best effort. Although they lose the overall race, they still strive to win. The coach has successfully "framed" the race to achieve a positive result.

Losing a game is a failure—but it also represents a great teaching moment. If a coach frames the loss as a lesson learned, and practices to overcome the problem, his or her players will also view the loss as a necessary part of growing and becoming better players. Likewise, when playing a superior opponent, a coach can cast his team in the role of the underdog—and emphasize the opportunity for his players to play their best and relish the challenge of possibly upsetting their more talented opponent.

If you're a non-coaching parent, look for coaches who employ the positive approach to coaching discussed above. Not only will they provide excellent instruction, but also engage your child in a way that builds self-esteem, confidence, and a joy for the game itself.

2) Parents as providers

As mentioned earlier, parents often play multiple roles within youth sports including team coach, supportive fan, as well as personal advisor, coach, and provider. We've already discussed the coaching role. Let's now take a closer look at parents in their provider role and how their actions can either help or hurt their child's experience in youth sports.

Supply the basics (opportunity and equipment)

For your child to participate in youth sports you must first provide him or her with the *opportunity* to play. In organized sports, this means signing-up your child, paying any required fee, and transporting your child to and from practices and games. For younger children just starting out, you will likely need to promote participation in the organized sport to your child.

Also consider how you affect your child's opportunity to participate in self-directed play, including neighborhood pickup games. In years gone by, parents would kick their kids outside in the summer to go and play with their friends (often to play sports). With two paycheck families and parent's heightened concern about safety, this childhood opportunity for summertime play is less prevalent. And with numerous electronic options to fill their spare time, children are hardly pushing their parents to let them go outside and play with other children. As discussed in *Step 1: Balance self-directed play and organized sports*, you still should provide your child with this opportunity for self-directed play. Depending on your personal situation and concerns, you may need to work at finding acceptable opportunities for your child to enjoy self-directed play.

Along with the opportunity to play, a child needs the basic equipment of the sport in which they participate. Some organized youth sports such as soccer, basketball, and flag football require little in the way of equipment expense. A good pair of shoes and ball will enable any child to play, practice, and explore their passion for the sport. These team sports are usually well supported within a community and your child should have easy access to developmental leagues and skill clinics.

Other team sports such as hockey, lacrosse and tackle football usually require a larger investment in equipment on the part of parents (although the cost is sometimes defrayed by the youth sport organization itself).

Individual sports such as golf, tennis, and skiing not only have an equipment expense but may also require that you invest in personal lessons for your child. Access to free instruction in these sports is usually more limited than youth team sports.

Support, encourage, and convey values

Your child has signed up for an organized sport, you've provided him or her with the necessary equipment, and the team seems to have a good coach. Now it's time for you to provide the support and encouragement your child will need as they go through the ups and downs of the season.

Children enjoy their parents taking a positive interest in their sports activities. Listen to their stories, congratulate them on their successes no matter how small, and attend their games whenever possible. Despite the hassles of modifying your family's routine and transporting your child, stay positive and don't make your child feel guilty about the sacrifices you are possibly making.

When your child is discouraged or plays poorly, listen first. A few key words or ideas from you may be all that's needed to make your child feel better. Framing your child's concern in a different light may help bring it into proper perspective. If the issue is related to your child's sports skills, propose spending some time together to overcome your son or daughter's skill deficiencies. Other options, such as personal lessons, may also help your child overcome skill related issues. If your child enjoys his or her sport, and is intent on improving, do your best to keep your child's hopes alive. Don't tell your child he or she is not good enough. There's time enough later on for a realistic appraisal of your child's future in any given sport.

Finally, send the right messages to your children. Promote positive goals. Emphasize having fun, striving to be your best, sportsmanship, accountability, and learning from one's mistakes. Don't accept destructive behavior and thought patterns. For example, if you hear complaints about the referees or coaches, don't let your child play the victim role. Instead, tell your child to concentrate on the parts of the game they control. When mistakes are made, suggest to your child that he or she translate any negative energy into positive actions like playing with more intensity and focus.

Avoid parental behavior traps

You're a passenger on your child's journey through youth sports—with the opportunity to either make the passage go more smoothly or cause a wreck. If you follow the principles advocated in this book, your child will enjoy sports, achieve at a higher level, gain more self-esteem, and likely continue playing sports as an adult.

Most parents naturally do a great job shepherding their child through youth sports. But there are many temptations that parents face that can derail their child's success in sports. One trap that can snare unsuspecting parents is living vicariously through their child's sports experiences—and basing their own sense of worth on their child's successes or failures. This leads to dysfunctional behavior for both parents and their children. To achieve success, parents may place an emphasis on the sport that far exceeds the natural interest of the child. The child, in turn, develops a distorted perspective of sports, and may improperly relate success in sports to his or her parent's love.

Parents also too often see sports as a vehicle to reach some external reward such as a college scholarship. Despite strong statistics to the contrary, parents readily believe that their young sports star is on the fast track to a scholarship. Too much emphasis is again placed on sports with the resulting cascade of behaviors that lead to the child eventually quitting sports.

Here are some potentially harmful parental behaviors to avoid:

- *Defining success only as winning (win/no-win).* Conveying a "Winners win and Losers lose" value may destroy the intrinsic rewards that help drive your child's long-term participation in sports.

- *Beyond introducing your child to a sport, forcing participation.* The goal is for your child to find his or her passion—not yours. This may take a child in a direction away from sports and your expectations.

- *Viewing sports as a waste of time with no practical real-world value (and discouraging your child's participation).* Similar to the above item, a parent's attitudes may neglect the child's true nature.

- *Becoming too involved in your child's sports experience.* Whatever the motivation (caring, vicarious enjoyment, parental status, etc.), over-involvement can diminish or ruin your child's independent enjoyment of his or her sport.

- *Continually blaming others for your child's disappointments and setbacks.* Attributing every negative situation to poor coaching or officiating promotes a destructive "victim" mentality in your child.

- *Coaching your child from the sidelines.* Constant interaction with your child during a game can diminish a child's confidence and self-reliance.

3) Players as students

While coaches and parents provide instruction and support, this is only one side of the coin that buys a great youth sports experience. Children must also contribute their share. As a parent, you need to help your child understand his or her responsibilities while also creating conditions favorable to achieving them. Let's take a look at two key responsibilities, along with some other positive behaviors that your child should ideally adopt.

Ready to have fun

First, your child should be ready to have fun! Most children are playful by nature and want to engage in physical activity with other children. But challenges are ever-present for a developing child, and there are many potential impediments to having fun. Less athleticism than other children, playing with older kids, peer pressure, participating in organized sports for the first time, and poor coaching can all test a child's attitude toward playing sports. Undue parental pressure and expectations can also hurt a child's desire to play sports. Helping your child maintain a proper perspective about his or her successes and failures is essential.

As a child develops, gains more experience, and better understands how to succeed, he or she should naturally enjoy playing the game—in all of its aspects. Fun and other internal rewards intrinsic to the actual play will drive the child's desire to participate. The child will enjoy not only games, but also practicing.

On the other hand, a child who is disinterested and rarely laughs, despite positive coaching and parental support, may simply not enjoy playing the sport. If this is the case, his or her passion may lie in another sport or an entirely different area (music, theatre, academics).

A desire to learn

The second essential characteristic is a child's desire to learn new skills and improve. If a child's prior experience in sports is relatively untarnished, this trait should be alive and well. Within a supportive environment, he or she will naturally enjoy learning and mastering new skills. Exposure to constant failure or negative parenting/coaching, however, may render the child less hopeful. He or she may be less willing to expend energy on a seemingly futile endeavor. Fearful of making embarrassing mistakes and lacking confidence, the child will walk away from sports at the first opportunity.

A child's desire to learn is the engine that helps power an individual down the road to self-improvement. With each milestone, the child's success becomes greater and his or her interest in continuing to play a sport becomes more established. But just as engines breakdown if not properly maintained, so can your child's attitude toward learning. Too many games in an organized sports season, poor coaching, too much parental pressure, and situations in which your child is continually overmatched, are all factors that can destroy your child's natural desire to learn and improve. Do your best to find the balance that protects this valuable asset.

Sharing the play

Coaches and parents should also look to promote other positive attributes. Each child should understand the importance of sharing the play with his or her teammates. Although a few children will succeed in an independent starring role, most others will find success by understanding how to individually perform well—*and* make their teammates better (thus adding even more value to the team).

Facing adversity

Children also need to understand that they will face adversity in their journey through youth sports. Learning how to cope with obstacles in life is part of every child's development. But they should also learn that meeting and surpassing the more difficult challenges provides greater reward. This can be either an internal sense of satisfaction or a more tangible external reward (trophy, praise, etc.). Children should also come to understand that not all rewards are realized in the short term.

Respect

Early on, young players must learn to respect coaches, teammates, opponents, officials, the rules of the game, and themselves. Each of these helps form the sports experience.

In team sports, success is most often based on the collective efforts of many players and a coach. Each participant plays a different role. Each should respect and acknowledge the other's contributions, and where possible, help enable others to more effectively play their role. *Great* players make their teammates better.

Opponents are part of the same community, sharing similar values and goals. Each opponent provides the competition that can potentially bring out the best in the other. Children should learn to always respect their opponent.

The game and its rules must also be respected. Sports are essentially structured play, where participants agree to adhere to a set of rules that both define the game and promote fair competition. Cheating or "bending the rules" during a contest undermines this structure—sometimes to the point where the competition itself is ruined.

And finally, young athletes should respect themselves. Maintaining a healthy body and mind through good habits is essential to realizing one's potential, finding happiness, and enjoying a full life of participation in sports.

AFTERWORD

Earlier in this book, I used the phrase "Start slow—finish strong" to help describe how a coach should build his or her team through the course of a season. It's worth emphasizing that this phrase is one that parents should also keep in mind as they mold their child's youth sports experience.

Laying the proper foundation of opportunity, knowledge and fun—one that provides both short and long-term benefits—is a gift that will benefit your child throughout his or her lifetime. In your desire to see your child succeed, strive to maintain a perspective that is in keeping with your child's own passion and place in his or her journey.

If you have found the ideas within this book helpful, and want to learn more, I invite you to visit www.insideyouthsports.org. This website contains additional articles that will help you create a great sports experience for your child.

ACKNOWLEDGEMENTS

Our youth reflects the contributions of so many around us. Family, teachers, friends (and antagonists), all play their role in helping to form the experience that is our childhood. The joy that sports have brought into my life certainly is the result of these individual's contributions, as is the approach to youth sports that I present within this book. With a special thanks to my parents and coaches, I am grateful to all.

Even a short book, such as this one, requires the help of others. I would like to thank all of my friends who read early drafts, suggested improvements, and offered their support for this project.

NOTES

NOTES

7523384R0

Made in the USA
Lexington, KY
03 December 2010